Introduction to Computer Programming
By Derek Felsher

About the Author

Derek Felsher, born in 1969, is a computer programmer from Johannesburg, South Africa. He has a Bachelor of Science from the University of Cape Town, is a qualified SAP Consultant in 2 disciplines (ABAP, B1) and has been involved in programming for almost 20 years. Three of these years were spent as a computer programming lecturer (where he realized the necessity for this book). Over the years he has been exposed to many programming languages including COBOL, C, Coldfusion (Internet Programming), SQL, DB2, CICS, ABAP and others. He has been exposed to programming in the Banking, Insurance, Mining and Financial Services industries.

Author's Foreword

BOOK I

This is a simple, practical book that anyone can understand. It is written to talk the reader through the wonderful world of computer programming.

When I was a lecturer at a computer programming school, we always allowed the students that *did not* pass the course, to redo the course for free. It always turned out that these repeat students achieved the highest marks in the class. **WHY?**

The students battled first time round because they couldn't **grasp** the **concept** of the programming tool being taught at that moment. To complicate matters further, they also had to learn to apply the tool in the correct format (computer language). By the time they caught on, they were battling with the next concept, always **behind the class** and having a miserable time.

The reason for them achieving great marks the second time round is that they understood the **concepts** of programming. They understood the **fundamentals** of what programming languages can do and thereafter they just had to learn the rules on how to apply them. They could enjoy and master each next phase.

There are many different computer programming languages but generally, they all apply the same concepts. It's like telling a dog to fetch a bone either in English, or Chinese. You need to understand that the dog can fetch the bone.

This book is written in **layman's** terms throughout. There is no use of programming syntax – so anyone can follow. The aim of the book is to explain the **different tools** that are used to develop a program, that are **common to all computer programming languages**.

I have provided examples of what a program might look like for each concept. These examples are designed such that the reader is exposed to program design without knowing it. I also often throw into an example, a concept that is yet to be discussed, just to 'soften the blow'.

Once the **concepts** are understood the reader can then start learning programming with the confidence that they can keep up with the class, enjoy and excel.

Finally, I have written and rewritten each section numerous times, to try and get the explanation across in as few words as possible. I understand that time is of the essence for all of us, and therefore I believe the content can be grasped in a few short days.

BOOK II

Once you have completed BOOK I, you should have a good understanding of the concepts of programming. BOOK II expands on some of the concepts already covered. We dig a little deeper by throwing you into realistic programming scenarios.

I have also added a few career tips and insights which I have personally experienced through the school of 'hard knocks'. Please remember these ideas are my own personal opinion, and are not cast in stone.

Some of these chapters may require a re-read and a bit more effort, but like all things in life, what you put in – you will get out.

I just want to point out that 'Book I' covers all the essentials – this is just a little bit extra.

I hope you enjoy.

This book is suitable for the following readers:

- **School kids** embarking on (or currently in) a computer studies curriculum.
- **University students** embarking on (or currently in) a computer studies curriculum.
- **Students** about to do (or currently in) a computer programming course.
- People in the workforce changing or considering **changing careers** into the programming environment.
- Any person **curious** about what programming is and how programs are created.

AGE categories: **13 yrs** and above

I DEDICATED THIS BOOK TO MY DEAR WIFE, SHIBOLET AND PRECIOUS CHILDREN, ELIANA AND MEIR.

Table of contents

BOOK I

BOOK II

BOOK I

1) What is Programming?

Whenever we use any computer program, be it a computer game, an accounting package, a spreadsheet or programs written to do special functions, a computer programmer has written a computer program.

A **program** is a set of **INSTRUCTIONS** issued to the brain of the computer that carries out these instructions. The **programmer** decides what the instructions should be. The brain of the computer, known as the **CPU** (central processing unit), carries out these instructions, one by one.

In a nut shell, these instructions (a program) do 3 main things:

- Put information into the computer (via the keyboard)
- Do stuff with (manipulate) this information
- Get the information back out of the computer (screen, printer etc.)

… and it is the programmer's job to write a program to do this.

These instructions will be typed up into a single document, instruction by instruction. When the program runs, this document will be read by the computer brain, and each instruction will be processed until the end of the document is reached. Pretty much like a cooking recipe …

Use 1 a cup of water
Add a couple of eggs
Mix in a bit of sugar
Shake a couple of times
Bake for 5 minutes …

How does the programmer and the CPU (computer brain) understand each other? The programmer types in the instructions in a language similar to English. This is known as **source code**. Once all the source code is typed in, it is converted into a language the computer understands, known as **object code**.

Finally this object code is combined with 'already built in instructions' to create the program that runs, called **executable code**. Our main focus is to grasp the concepts, rules and tools of **source code**.

Again, programming is the science (and art), of "building" software that runs on computers. This software is made up of a program (or programs) which, in turn, are made up of a bunch of instructions.

People often say "... **the computer must automatically do this or that** ... ". I hope that after going through this book, you will understand that it is the programmer, with his/her programs, that make things **automatic**.

2) Storing data (memory)

Bits & Bytes

To understand programs, we need to 1st have some idea of how information is stored in the computer. First time round, you may find this a bit tricky, so my advice for this chapter (and the rest of the book) is to read slowly, and re-read if necessary.

The place we store data in is called **memory**. In our minds, we picture the data stored in computer memory as:

abcdefghijklmnopqrstuvwxyz1234567890!@#$%^&*()_+ABCDEFGHIJKLM
NOPQRSTUVWXYZ1+,./'\[]=-<>?|":}{

This memory however, is actually made up of millions of tiny magnets (yip, the ones we stick to our fridges). These tiny magnets can either be magnetized (i.e. stick 'on') or non-magnetized (i.e. do not stick 'off').

As you can now imagine, storage or, memory, is made up of millions of these little magnets, stacked adjacent to each other, looking something like this:

```
O●●OOOOO●O●OOOO●O●●OOOO●O●●OOO●O●●OOOO●
O●●OOO●O●●OOO●O●●OOO●O●●OOO●O●●OOOO●
O●●OO●O●●OOOO●O●●OOO●O●●OOO●O●●OOOO●
```

Combinations of these millions of magnets next to each other, some 'on' some 'off', are translated into meaningful data that the CPU can understand and work with.

Looking at the characters on our keyboard:

abcdefghijklmnopqrstuvwxyz1234567890!@#$%^&()_+ABCDEFGHIJKLM
NOPQRSTUVWXYZ1+,./'\[]=-<>?|":}{*

each one of the above characters is allocated **8 magnets**, some on '●' and some off 'O'.

```
'a' in storage = O●●OOOOO●
'b' in storage = O●●OOO●O
'Z' in storage = O●O●●O●O
```

Each magnet is called a **BIT**, and as described above, **8** bits grouped together to represent a character on the keyboard, is called a **BYTE**.

So:
- **1 character** (i.e. 'a') = 8 bits = 8 magnets = 1 byte.
- The name 'Shibolet' = 8 characters = 8 bytes (64 magnets: 8 magnets for 'S' another 8 magnets for 'h' and so on).
- The number '123' = 3 BYTES (24 magnets).
- 1 MB (we've all heard of Megabytes) = 1 Megabyte = 1,024,000 BYTES.

Binary code

This small chapter may seem a little mind boggling, but it will help us to visualize how the computer processes information (data). So let's try grasp as much as we can, although don't sweat it, it won't make or break you as a programmer.

The **language** used by the computer brain (CPU) to process meaning out of these magnets above is called '**BINARY CODE**'. BINARY CODE is made up of only two numbers '0' and '1'.

While we are thinking in terms of the characters on the keyboard (a,b,% etc..), the computer is thinking in '0's and '1's. Now each key on the keyboard has build under it tiny pipes, some open and some blocked. When you push a key, the open pipes send electric power and the closed pipes do not. Each part of the computer interprets these combinations of power/no-power (using '0' and '1' as the universal language). And this is how our combinations of 8 magnets are either switched on (magnetized) or not.

So, if a magnet is switched ON, the computer brain assigns the magnet a '0', and if the magnet is switched OFF, the computer brain assigns the magnet a '1'. Putting it all together,

'a' in storage = O●●OOOOO● is processed in the CPU as 01100001
'b' in storage = O●●OOOO●O is processed in the CPU as 01100010
'Z' in storage = O●O●●O●O is processed in the CPU as 01011010

How does the CPU know which letter or key on the keyboard is represented in computer language (Binary Code)? There is a *map* that we follow that matches each key on the keyboard to 8 BITS, either on or off.

As a programmer, you will not need to know what data looks like in Binary Code. This is only for the super-bright. All you need to know is how many bytes are being used, and what these bytes represent in "keyboard" language.

3) Records, Fields and Files/Tables

In this chapter we will try **break down** this information storage into a format that we can better understand. This stuff is a bit more important than the previous chapter, so try your best to follow.

Records

Let's pretend it is the good ol' days before computers were invented. Imagine a school, whose secretary has the responsibility of keeping records of all the pupils.

She would take a card for each student and write on the card the following information:

Pupil Name:	*Mary Jane*
Birth Date:	*03 Dec 1979*
Address:	*01 5th Street Melrose*

Another card might contain:

Pupil Name:	*John Smith*
Birth Date:	*14 Feb 1969*
Address:	*08 12th Street Illovo*

… and so on, for each student.

She would then file each card in the filing cabinet.

Computers, store data in a similar fashion.

Just like the written cards, the computer would group data together for each student, where each group of …

    - Pupil Name
    - Birth Date
    - Address

... is called a **RECORD**, i.e.

RECORD 1	RECORD 2
Pupil Name: **Mary Jane**	Pupil Name: **John Smith**
Birth Date: **03 Dec 1979**	Birth Date: **04 Feb 1969**
Address: **01 5TH Street**	Address: **08 12th Avenue**

In memory, these records are stored one next to the other.

Applying what we learnt earlier, the records sit next to each other as magnets:

O●●OOOO●O●OOOO●O●●OOOO●O●●OOO●O●●OOOO●

but understood by the computer in binary language:

01100001010000101100001011011101011000001

Our 2 records, once converted from binary to 'our language', could be imagined as follows:

Mary Jane 03 Dec 1979 01 5th Street John Smith Feb 1969 08 12th Avenue….

Do you notice how muddled up the data looks because it is one long string of characters.

1. *How does the program know where each record starts and ends?*
2. *How does it know which characters form part of 'PUPIL NAME' and which characters form part of 'BIRTH DATE'?*

Answer. We need to **'define the structure'** of our records.

Fields

Each 'record' is divided up into different **FIELDS**. Each **field** represents a different **type** of data e.g.

PUPIL NAME - is a **field** that contains "name" data

BIRTH DATE - is a **field** containing "birth date" data

ADDRESS - is a **field** containing "address" data

We will refer to these specific **fields** later in our program when we want to specifically address the 'NAME' or 'ADDRESS' in a specific record.

In the drawing below, notice how we have data for 3 records, with each record having Fields: Pupil, Birth Date and Address.

	Pupil	Birth Date	Address
Record 1	Mary Smith	14 Jan 1995	19 4th Str
Record 2	John Dims	10 Jul 1996	05 6th Ave
Record 3	Gary Long	01 May 1994	23 9th Ave

Now, let's say the school also needs to keep information or records of its **teachers**. We would have a whole new set of teacher records, with **fields** relating to teachers i.e.

Teacher Record

Field1: TEACHER NAME
Field2: CLASS
Field3: SALARY

In the drawing below, notice how we have data for 3 records, with each record having Fields: Teacher, Class and Salary.

	Teacher	Class	Salary
Record 1	Mrs. Bate	Grade 5	$3000
Record 2	Mr. Smith	Grade 8	$4000
Record 3	Mrs. Jeeves	Grade 3	$2000

Continuing along this line, let's say the school also needs to keep information or records of its **classrooms**. We would have a whole new set of classroom records, with **fields** relating to classrooms i.e.

Classroom Record

Field1: CLASSROOM NAME
Field2: NUMBER OF SEATS
Field3: LOCATION

In the drawing below, notice how we have data for 3 records, with each record having Fields: Name, No. of Seats and Location.

	Name	No. of Seats	Location
Record 1	Green Class	30	Upstairs C1
Record 2	Blue Class	25	Downstairs B2
Record 3	Red Class	29	Upstairs C2

Files/Tables

Remember, we have to define what the records look like to the program. But, we have 2 different types of records, storing different types of data. Surely it would **not**

make sense to bunch all the "Pupil" data together with all the "Teacher" data. It would be all mixed up, and how would the computer differentiate between the two?

It would make sense to separate our different types of records, into different areas in storage (memory). These separate areas in storage that contain records of the same data, are called **FILES** or **TABLES**. Like a draw in a filing cabinet, for different cards. The best way to picture these files/tables in storage is as we described above,

PUPIL FILE/TABLE

	Pupil	Birth Date	Address
Record 1	Mary Smith	14 Jan 1995	19 4th Str
Record 2	John Dims	10 Jul 1996	05 6th Ave
Record 3	Gary Long	01 May 1994	23 9th Ave

TEACHER FILE/TABLE

	Teacher	Class	Salary
Record 1	Mrs. Bate	Grade 5	$3000
Record 2	Mr. Smith	Grade 8	$4000
Record 3	Mrs. Jeeves	Grade 3	$2000

As programmers, we would need to give these FILES/TABLES there own names, so we could refer to them in the programs. Our programs would then call on the file/table to access the data in the records, or store new information, or change information.

We will discuss these files/tables in more detail later, but for now, in order to understand how our data will be **stored**, we need to:

1. List (define) our Fields that make up our records.
2. List (define) our Files/Tables that store these records.

From now on we would like to demonstrate the concepts we cover by including them in an actual program. To do this, our goal will be to write a computer program for a school. The program will capture, change and display pupil and teacher information.

LET'S START BUILDING OUR PROGRAM (INSTRUCTIONS):

PROGRAM NAME: SCHOOL DATA	
FILES/TABLES USED: PUPIL DATA, TEACHER DATA	
PUPIL DATA FIELDS	**TEACHER DATA FIELDS**
- pupil	- teacher
- birth date	- grade
- address	- salary
- math mark (score)	
- English mark (score)	

Note 1. Each program must have its own unique name **'PROGRAM NAME'** *that differentiates it from other programs, and gives some idea of what the program is actually doing.*

4) Operating Systems and Temporary Storage

When our programs request usage of a file in storage, the tool that actually does the work, or 'makes this happen' is the OPERATING SYSTEM.

The OPERATING SYSTEM is also a bunch of programs that acts as GO BETWEEN, for our program instructions and the data being used in the files.

Think of a football match where both teams sit in their own change rooms before the game, they are brought together to interact on the field, and then go back to their change rooms.

In computer terms, the programs and Data (files/tables) sit in storage (the change rooms) before being used. When the program runs, the operating system, moves both the *file/table data* and the *program instructions* to an area where they can play together (the field), and then once finished, sends them back.

The change room in computer terms would be PERMANENT STORAGE (ever heard of a hard drive?)

The football field in computer terms would be TEMORARY STORAGE (ever heard of RAM).

If you have ever overheard people talking about a 40 Gig Hard Drive, or 1 Gigs of RAM, they are talking about how many bytes can be stored in **permanent** or temporary storage.

The details of how operating systems work is not for this book. You just need to know that a 'whole bunch of stuff' goes on behind the scenes to get programs to run. Our programs use the screens, the printers, the keyboard, the speakers etc. All this coordination is controlled by the 'operating system'.

5) Input and Output

We will now introduce the terms **INPUT** and **OUTPUT**, that are used constantly in data processing and represents the movement of data 'into' or 'out of' the computer.

There are really only 4 things we can do to data.

1) **ADD (WRITE)** data to a file/table - *output*
2) **VIEW (READ)** data from a file/table - *input*
3) **CHANGE** data in a file/table
4) **REMOVE (DELETE)** data from a file/table

Output

When we add data or records to a file/table, we say we are **WRITING a record** to the file/table - this is considered 'output'.

When we view data or records that exist in a file/table we say we are **READING a record** - this is considered **'input'**.

Question: How do we record or 'WRITE' all the pupil records into the PUPIL DATA file, in other words, how do we get all that stuff in there?

Answer: Using our keyboard, we 'OUTPUT' the data to the file/table.

  - simply put ... we **type**: 'Mary Jane' and hit 'ENTER'.

The program we are using to do this, might then display on the screen: **'Please Capture next Pupil'**.

This message is also considered **'OUTPUT'**, as we have written (output) the message to the screen.

So to capture a file full of records, our program could look like this:

PROGRAM NAME: CAPTURE PUPILS
FILES/TABLES USED: PUPIL DATA
PUPIL DATA FIELDS
- pupil
- birth date
- address
- math mark
- English mark
PROGRAM WORK
Display on Screen 'Enter next pupil details or Esc to Exit' (output)
WRITE data to Pupil File/Table (output)
Display on Screen 'Enter next pupil details or Esc to Exit'
WRITE data to Pupil File/Table
Display on Screen 'Enter next pupil details or Esc to Exit'
WRITE data to Pupil File/Table

Note 1. The `'PROGRAM WORK'` is used to tell the CPU that we have defined our Fields/Records/Files/Tables and we are ready to start the actual processing.

Note 2. We have not defined the TEACHER DATA file/table above because this particular program only uses PUPIL DATA.

Note 3. All good programmers place comments in their programs to add information that might be valuable to other programmers that might come along and make changes later. We will put our comments in ().

Note 4. As mentioned above, the program runs in temporary storage and writes the records to permanent storage.

Input

Now if we are *reading* records from a file, this is called **`'INPUT'`**. *We would read records from a file/table to draw on its information* **(input)**.

Let's say our program wants to see how many records there are in the file/table and then display the answer on the screen. The code might look like this:

...
PROGRAM WORK
READ a record (input)
add 1 to the total
READ next record (input)
add 1 to the total
READ next record (input)
add 1 to the total
display the total on the screen (output)

Input-Output

Let's say the school teacher wants to go through each pupil in the Pupil File/Table and give each pupil an extra 5% on their math mark.

We would read each record (input), add 5% to the math mark (in temporary storage), and then write each record back (output) to the file/table with the new math mark. We call the 'writing back', **REWRITING as it is the same record**. This is called **input-output**.

Our program would look like this:

...
PROGRAM WORK
READ a record (input)
ADD 5% to math mark
REWRITE record back (output)
READ next record (input)
ADD 5% to math mark
REWRITE record back (output)
READ next record (input)
ADD 5% to math mark
REWRITE record back (output)

How does the computer know where each file starts and ends? How does the computer know what the records look like in each file? That brings us to the next chapter …

6) Defining Fields

Remember, all files/tables are different, containing different fields, with different information. Therefore records of one file/table can be larger or smaller than records of another file/table. We must therefore **describe** each file/table to the computer operating system, so that when the program requests to:

READ a record …

the correct number of **BYTES** are read, making up the full record. Likewise, when we create a file we need to tell the operating system how many bytes to use when sending the information down to permanent storage.

All programs define files/tables in a similar fashion. At the top of the program we would say something like this:

THE FILENAME IS CALLED 'PUPIL DATA'
EACH RECORD HAS THE FOLLOWING FIELDS:
NAME (40 bytes)
ENGLISH mark (5 bytes)
MATH mark (5 bytes)

As you can see the total bytes of the record = 50 bytes (40 + 5 + 5).

Now when you say 'READ A RECORD', the operating system knows to go fetch 50 BYTES of memory at a time (50 X 8 magnets). When you READ the first record, it goes to BYTE number 1 of the file, and counts 50 BYTES from there to move. When you READ the next record it goes to BYTE 51 of the file, and counts 50 BYTES from there, and so on.

This can be demonstrated in **DELETING RECORDS** as well.

Let's say a pupil leaves the school. We would not need to keep the data (unless required). We would need a mechanism to remove the record from the file/table. We could say:

DELETE pupil 'Mary Smith' data record.

Can you see how important it is to know the size of each record. Only the 50 BYTES belonging to 'Mary Smith' must be deleted, and not some or the entire next pupil as well.

More about Field Descriptions

Let's say we have read a record from PUPIL FILE, and we now ONLY want to display the 'NAME' field. Where in the *50 BYTES*, do we find the *NAME* data?

We now need to split the record up, describing how many bytes each FIELD is, so that if you say:

| READ RECORD |
| DISPLAY **'NAME'** ON SCREEN |

… it knows which BYTES of the record to move to the screen. The computer doesn't know that 'DAVE' is a name and to stop displaying after the letter 'E'.

So we say in our program: *note the comments ()*

THE FILENAME IS CALLED 'PUPIL FILE'		
EACH RECORD HAS THE FOLLOWING FIELDS:		
NAME	20 BYTES	(bytes 1-20 *big enough to store a name*)
BIRTH DATE	10 BYTES	(bytes 21-30 could store yyyy/mm/dd)
ADDRESS	50 BYTES	(bytes 31-80 could store address details)
ENGLISH mark	3 BYTES	(bytes 81-83 must cater for 100%)
MATH mark	3 BYTES	(bytes 84-86)

If storage looked like this:

         DAVE SMITH   1969/02/14 …
BYTE *NO:*   *1234567890123456789012345678901 23456* …
         1   10   20   30

and we say 'DISPLAY **NAME** ON SCREEN', the operating system sees the above definition, that NAME is stored in bytes 1-20, and moves those exact 20 bytes to the screen i.e. *DAVE SMITH*

If we say 'DISPLAY **BIRTH DATE** ON SCREEN', the system sees the above definition, that BIRTH DATE = bytes 21-30 and pops those bytes on the screen i.e. *1969/02/14*

So we have to define each field in each record so the operating system understands **exactly** what it is dealing with when it READS, WRITES or manipulates data.

Types of fields

When we define these fields at the top of the program, we also need to specify what **type** of data these fields are storing. In a nutshell, we need to specify whether the field holds NUMBERS or LETTERS or BOTH.

Therefore we have:

```
        NUMERIC fields        (0-9)
        ALPHABETIC fields     (A-Z)
        ALPHANUMERIC fields   (A-Z,0-9,/<.,":]\-=)
        GROUP fields
```

NUMERIC fields are made up of numbers only. It is always necessary to state how many decimal places the number might contain.

ALPHABETIC fields contain letters of the alphabet.
ALPHANUMERIC fields contain any key you see on the keyboard, i.e. numbers, letters, and all the other symbols like:
                ` < > ? { etc.

Our school records would now look like this:

FILE: 'PUPIL FILE'	
NAME	20 bytes, Alphabetic
BIRTH-DATE	10 bytes, Alphanumeric (stores yyyy/mm/dd)
ADDRESS	50 bytes, Alphanumeric
MATH mark	3 bytes, Numeric
ENGLISH mark	3 bytes, Numeric

*Can you see that for the MATH mark we **cannot** store '75%' because the '%' is not a number. If we wanted to store 75% we would have to define the field as ALPHANUMERIC. Therefore we only store 75.*

Alignment of Fields

It is important to always cater for the maximum space needed for each field. If we made **NAME** 3 bytes then most names would not fit in that field. Likewise for **MATH mark**, if we made it 2 bytes, we could not store 100.

The question is, 'what happens to those extra bytes if they are not all used up?'

e.g. **NAME = 'David Smith'** = 11 bytes, but the field is defined to store 20 bytes.

If the field is ALPHABETIC or ALPHANUMERIC, then the extra bytes are filled with **spaces** at the **end**.

So **NAME** would contain in storage:

```
BYTE:12345678901234567890
     DAVID SMITH
```

Note how the spaces are fitted at the end. It would be wise to remember that space or ' ' is actually stored as a character, just like the letter 'a' or 'b'.

If it is a **NUMERIC** field, then those extra bytes are automatically filled with **zeroes**. The difference with numeric fields is that the zeroes are stored in the **front**.

I.E. if a numeric field defined to store 3 bytes has a value in it of **77**, then that value is stored as **077**. If we defined a 5 bytes, Numeric, then it would be stored as **00077**. Note again how the zeroes are always in front.

7) Using Fields

Getting Data from the Keyboard

If we want to insert data into a field we have to get it from somewhere. Sometimes data is entered from the keyboard.

Our code would look like this: (forget about tables for now)

DISPLAY ON THE SCREEN 'ENTER NAME'
MAKE THE FIELD 'NAME' **EQUAL** TO WHATEVER IS TYPED IN
DISPLAY ON THE SCREEN 'ENTER ENGLISH marks'
MAKE THE FIELD 'ENGLISH marks' **EQUAL** TO WHATEVER IS TYPED IN
DISPLAY ON THE SCREEN 'ENTER MATH marks'
MAKE THE FIELD 'MATH marks' **EQUAL** TO WHATEVER IS TYPED IN

Different languages have shortened ways of saying:

MAKE THE FIELD 'NAME' **EQUAL** TO WHATEVER IS TYPED IN

Most languages however, will define 'NAME' to temporary storage and then say something like:

PUT INTO NAME

This would need an instruction 1st to tell the user what to do i.e.

DISPLAY ON THE SCREEN 'ENTER NAME'
PUT INTO NAME

This will actually look like this on the screen:

```
┌─────────────────────────────────┐
│                                 │
│     ENTER NAME  _____      │
│                                 │
└─────────────────────────────────┘
```

The _____ is telling the user to enter data and when the user enters data, the statement 'PUT INTO NAME', will send the data from the keyboard to the field 'NAME' in temporary storage.

Using the above knowledge, we can now say:

PROGRAM NAME: DISPLAY-STUDENT	
TEMPORARY STORAGE	
NAME	20 bytes, Alphabetic
ENGLISH mark	3 bytes, Numeric
MATH mark	3 bytes, Numeric
PROGRAM START	
DISPLAY 'ENTER NAME'	
PUT INTO NAME	
DISPLAY 'ENTER ENGLISH marks'	
PUT INTO ENGLISH mark	
DISPLAY 'ENTER MATH marks'	
PUT INTO MATH mark	

Moving Data

Sometimes we need to make the contents of one field equal to the contents of another field. We could say:

```
MOVE THE CONTENTS OF FIELD1 INTO FIELD2
```

Sometimes we need to **initialize** a field to a value i.e.

```
SET NAME TO "JAMES"
SET COUNT TO 0
```

Arithmetic

We can do arithmetic **on** fields and **between** fields. All arithmetic done on a calculator can be done with fields. Most languages allow you to specify your code in math format i.e.

```
FIELD1 = FIELD2 + FIELD3
FIELD1 = FIELD5 / FIELD6 ( '/' is usually used for 'divide')
TOTAL = COUNT * MATH marks ('*' is usually used for 'multiply')
```

or English format i.e.

```
ADD THE CONTENTS OF FIELD2 TO FIELD3
DIVIDE FIELD5 BY FIELD6
MULTIPLY FIELD4 BY 6
```

Temporary Storage Fields

We have dealt with the fields used to define records in files/tables. These files/tables are kept in permanent storage (the change rooms), and brought into temporary storage (the football pitch) to be worked on by the program. Sometimes **'worker fields'**, not belonging to any file/table, are required in temporary storage to help us do work. They are just there to help us manipulate data where needed.

Let's say we want *to count how many records there are in a file*. Where would we **hold** this *count*, as it does not belong to any of the file/table records?

We would define a field called 'COUNT' to temporary storage. It would be defined the same way:

i.e. COUNT   5 bytes, Numeric.

our program would look like this:

PROGRAM NAME: COUNT PUPILS
FILE: PUPIL FILE
NAME   20 bytes, Alphabetic
BIRTH-DATE   10 bytes, Alphanumeric (stores yyyy/mm/dd)
ADDRESS   50 bytes, Alphanumeric
MATH mark   3 bytes, Numeric
ENGLISH mark   3 bytes, Numeric
TEMPORARY STORAGE
COUNT   5 bytes, numeric
PROGRAM START
READ a record (input)
ADD 1 to **COUNT**
Have we read all records? NO (explained later)
READ next record (input)
ADD 1 to **COUNT**
Have we read all records? NO
READ next record (input)
ADD 1 to **COUNT**
Have we read all records? YES
display **COUNT** on the screen (output)

When deciding on what name to give a field, we try our best to describe the data being stored (i.e. 'NAME' or 'SALARY').

The only words that cannot be used for field names are words that are used as part of the programming language (i.e. 'READ' or 'MOVE' or 'FILE'. These words are called 'RESERVED WORDS'.

Would it make sense to say: MOVE 'FIELD1' TO 'MOVE'?

Group Fields

Count the bytes in the below code.

STREET	50 bytes, Alphanumeric
SUBURB	50 bytes, Alpha…
CITY	50 bytes, Alpha…

Can you see how the above fields add up 150 bytes? Sometimes we want to do something with all 150 bytes at once. Perhaps we want to move or display all the bytes in one go.

We can rather define the 3 fields under a GROUP FIELD (ADDRESS)

ADDRESS (group filed)	
STREET	50 bytes, Alphanumeric
SUBURB	50 bytes, Alphanumeric
CITY	50 bytes, Alphanumeric

… and instead of saying: … we can say:

DISPLAY STREET	DISPLAY ADDRESS
DISPLAY SUBURB	
DISPLAY CITY	

Programs Crashing

Ever heard of a program *crashing*, or *aborting* or *abending*? This happens when something goes horribly wrong with the program, the computer doesn't know what to do, and the program just 'crashes'. It then spills out on the screen a huge about of jargon that only a professor can understand, and we usually end up rebooting our computers.

A number of things can cause this. One of these causes is fields holding data that they shouldn't be.

A typical example of this is when a NUMERIC field (which should contain numbers 0-9), actually ends up with 'non-numeric' data i.e. 'letters' or '^&%$@!'.

E.G. we have a field COUNT 5 bytes, numeric – containing `B1234A`. (note the non-numeric data in the field).

How can this be possible? There could be a number of reasons, but to illustrate the point we only need to look at 1.

TEMPORARY STORAGE	
COUNT	5 bytes, numeric

When our **program starts**, what do you think the field COUNT contains? The answer is 5 bytes of "rubbish".

If we try doing something with this field, i.e. arithmetic on it, **and it has rubbish, the program will crash/abort/abend.** When we SET COUNT to 1, it no longer contains "rubbish", but now contains 00001. We can now do arithmetic with `COUNT`.

8) Loops

We will now branch away from records and files and discuss a programming tool called LOOPS.

When the computer **does exactly the same thing** again and again and again and again and again and again and again and again and again and again and again … it is in a loop.

This is also known as **ITTERATIONS**.

This is necessary as sometimes we need the computer to repeat an action a number of times.

All languages make it possible to tell the computer to repeat something in an easy way.

The benefit of this is as follows:

Example 1.

If we want to read 1000 records, instead of saying:

Read record
Read next record
Read next record
Read next record
Read next record
Read next record
Read next record
Read next record
Read next record
Read next record
… and so on 1000 times

With the help of our **COUNT** field described above in temporary Storage, we can **rather** say:

SET THE COUNT TO 1
LOOP UNTIL COUNT > 1000
Read record
Add 1 to COUNT
LOOP END

Note how we place the stuff we want to repeat inside the:

LOOP
...
LOOP END

You see, the 'dumb' computer doesn't know what we 'clever' humans are trying to do. It just follows instructions. If you don't tell it when to STOP doing something it just carries on *LOOPING and LOOPING and LOOPING and LOOPING and LOOPING and LOOPING and LOOPING and LOOPING and LOOPING and LOOPING ...*

So, looking at our example, the CPU will do the following:

1) set the value of field COUNT = 1
2) is the COUNT > 10? NO
3) so read a record, and add 1 to the COUNT (COUNT NOW = 2)
4) is the COUNT > 10? NO
5) so read a record, and add 1 to the COUNT (COUNT NOW = 3)
6) is the COUNT > 10? NO
7) so read a record, and add 1 to the COUNT (COUNT NOW = 4)
8) ... and so on ...
9) is the COUNT > 10? NO
10) so read a record, and add 1 to the COUNT (COUNT NOW = 11)
11) is the COUNT > 10? **YES**
12) **STOP THE LOOP.**

We can put as many statements as we want inside the LOOP - LOOP END.

Example 2.

What if we want to read an entire file of 1 million records, and display each record?

READ 1st RECORD
LOOP UNTIL LAST RECORD READ
DISPLAY FIELDS
READ RECORD
LOOP END

The above loop will repeat:

DISPLAY FIELDS
READ RECORD

until we have read the last record in the file - beats writing it out 1 million times.

Example 3.

What if we want to read an entire file of 1 million records, but only display "Jimmy the Fish's" Math mark?

READ 1st RECORD
LOOP UNTIL NAME = "Jimmy the Fish"
READ RECORD
LOOP END
DISPLAY MATH mark

The above loop will repeat:

READ RECORD

until we have reached the record where the NAME = "Jimmy the Fish". Once the record is found, the loop will end, and we then display only his data.

Note how we 1st read a record, and then went into the loop. This is just good programming "design", as we are able to check the 1st record, before we start the loop. If the 1st record is "Jimmy the Fish", we would not want to go into the loop.

Example 4.

We can even put a loop within a loop (loopy-da-loop). When this happens we treat the middle loop just like any other code. When the middle loop finishes, we go back to the top of the outer loop and start again, until the outer loop is complete.

LOOP UNTIL ...
LOOP UNTIL ...
...
LOOP END
LOOP END

SET X TO 0
LOOP UNTIL X > 2
ADD 1 TO X
SET Y TO 0
LOOP UNTIL Y > 2
ADD 1 TO Y
END LOOP
END LOOP

To grasp the above code, follow the numbers from 1 to 20 below.

1. X=0
2. X=1   7. X=2   12. X=3
3. Y=0   8. Y=0   13. Y=0
4. Y=1   9.   Y=1   14. Y=1
5. Y=2   10. Y=2   15. Y=2
6. Y=3   11. Y=3   16. Y=3

Notice how we start the OUTER loop (2. and 3.), then process the INNER loop (4.5.6.), then go back to the OUTER loop (7.8.), then re-process the INNER loop (9.10.11) … and so on:

UNTIL BOTH CONDITIONS ARE MET i.e. X > 2 and Y > 2.

Endless Loops

Looking at the below code, can you notice something missing?

```
SET X TO 1
LOOP UNTIL X > 2
    DISPLAY X
ENDLOOP
```

Yip, you guessed it. There should be something like:

'Add 1 to X'   … inside the loop.

The condition **'LOOP UNTIL X > 2'** would never be met, as we are never increasing 'X'. The program would display '1' forever, until someone notices that 'Hey, this program is in an **Endless Loop'**. The only way to stop the loop is to shut the program down. **So beware of endless loops.**

9) Arrays

Defining Arrays

Now that we have learnt the "LOOP" trick, let's see how it can help us use ARRAYS.

Arrays are used for **field definitions** that are **repeated** a number of times, e.g. *name1, name2, name3* OR *mark1, mark2, mark3* etc.

Let's say we wanted to keep a record of **every** test done by **every** student in the PUPIL FILE/TABLE. Now stay with us here as this could get a bit tricky.

Let's say in the year there are 10 **tests** done per subject (10 Math tests and 10 English tests). Our File/Table definition **could** look like this (remember this is what **EACH** student record **could** look like):

FILE: PUPIL FILE	
NAME	20 bytes, Alphabetic
BIRTH-DATE	10 bytes, Alphanumeric
ADDRESS	50 bytes, Alphanumeric
MATH mark1	3 bytes, Numeric
MATH mark2	3 bytes, Numeric
MATH mark3	3 bytes, Numeric
MATH mark4	3 bytes, Numeric
MATH mark5	3 bytes, Numeric
MATH mark6	3 bytes, Numeric
MATH mark7	3 bytes, Numeric
MATH mark8	3 bytes, Numeric
MATH mark9	3 bytes, Numeric
MATH mark10	3 bytes, Numeric
ENGLISH mark1	3 bytes, Numeric
ENGLISH mark2	3 bytes, Numeric
ENGLISH mark3	3 bytes, Numeric
ENGLISH mark4	3 bytes, Numeric
ENGLISH mark5	3 bytes, Numeric
ENGLISH mark6	3 bytes, Numeric
ENGLISH mark7	3 bytes, Numeric
ENGLISH mark8	3 bytes, Numeric
ENGLISH mark9	3 bytes, Numeric
ENGLISH mark10	3 bytes, Numeric

In storage, the bytes will look like this (note how a new name is the start of a new record):

John … 14/02/1969 North Street … 077 084 091 087 100 077 089 083 065 077 076 088 066 044 089 055 044 077 100 100 **Steven** … 15/03/1968 Plein Street … 088 099 055 077 055 077 078 065 … **Mary** … and so on.

Looking again at our definition can you see how tedious the exercise was of defining the marks. There is an easier and quicker way of doing this, **and the bytes in storage would look exactly the same.**

Because each field describing a mark is:

1) the same size in bytes (3)
2) the same type (numeric)

we can define the field **once for MATH, once for ENGLISH,** and we can say **'they occur 10 times'**. This is called an **ARRAY** of the same field. Our definition would look something like this:

MATH mark	3 bytes, Numeric **OCCURS 10**
ENGLISH mark	3 bytes, Numeric **OCCURS 10**

This means that there are 10 of the field ENGLISH mark, and 10 of the field MATH mark. It is important to understand that in storage these 20 fields will still sit next to each other, taking up 20 X 3 = 60 consecutive BYTES of memory, as described above.

Some languages also call these TABLES (different to a FILE/TABLE).

The obvious question is 'how do we know which ENGLISH or MATH mark we are dealing with when we are manipulating the data in our program?'.

Using Arrays

If we want to refer to the first *'Math Mark'* of a record, we simply say: **Math mark (1)**. If we want to refer to the 7th *'English Mark'*, we code: **English mark (7)**.

DISPLAY ON THE SCREEN MATH Mark(1)
Or
MOVE FIELDA TO ENGLISH Mark(7)

We can also use a numeric field 'X' that is defined in temporary storage.

DISPLAY MATH Mark(X)

Whatever value is in 'X' will be displayed, so if: X=1 this would be the same as math mark(1).

Now using **loops,** and **arrays,** we can get clever:

X=1
LOOP UNTIL X > 10
DISPLAY MATH Mark(X)
ADD 1 to X
END LOOP

That beats saying:

DISPLAY MATH Mark(1)
DISPLAY MATH Mark(2)
DISPLAY MATH Mark(3)
DISPLAY MATH Mark(4)
DISPLAY MATH Mark(5)
...

Imagine doing that for 50 Marks?

Let's use what we have learnt so far and build some code.

What if you want to read **each** record of the file and display **each** mark on the screen. (**Now** we talking programming).

PROGRAM NAME: DISPLAY PUPILS
FILE: PUPIL FILE
NAME   20 bytes, Alphabetic
BIRTH-DATE   10 bytes, Alphanumeric (stores yyyy/mm/dd)
ADDRESS   50 bytes, Alphanumeric
MATH mark   3 bytes, Numeric **OCCURS 10**
ENGLISH mark   3 bytes, Numeric **OCCURS 10**
TEMPORARY STORAGE
Count   3 bytes, numeric
PROGRAM START
READ RECORD FROM PUPIL FILE   (read 1st record)
LOOP UNTIL ALL RECORDS READ (start outer loop)
SET Count TO 1
LOOP UNTIL Count > 10 (start inner loop)
Display MATH mark (Count)
Display ENGLISH mark (Count)
ADD 1 to Count
END LOOP
READ RECORD FROM PUPIL FILE
END LOOP

Notice how we:
- read a record
- display marks (1-10) for MATH and ENGLISH
- read another record
- display marks (1-10) for MATH and ENGLISH
… and so on until we have reached the end of file.

HOW DO WE KNOW WHEN WE HAVE READ ALL RECORDS IN THE FILE?

*Files in storage are set up so that there is always an **End Of File** 'label' or 'indicator'. Once we read the last record, the next read after that will read the 'indicator'.*

Our file/table contains:
Record 1
Record 2
…
Record 1001
Record 1002
EOF (End of File)

*In most languages we need to check for this indicator (i.e. 'LOOP UNTIL ALL RECORDS READ'). If we do not have this check, and we carry on reading **past the end of file**, our program will CRASH.*

Hence we often see the following code:

```
LOOP UNTIL EOF (End Of File)
   DISPLAY RECORD
   READ NEXT RECORD
END LOOP
```

2 Dimensional Arrays

If you up for a bit of challenge, try get this bit on 2 dimensional arrays, but if it goes over your head, don't sweat it.

When you buy a ticket at the movies, and you are shown which seats are available in the cinema, you are looking at a 2 dimensional table.

```
    1 2 3 4 5 6
A   y y y y y y
B   y n y y y y
C   y y y n y y
D   y y y y n y
E   y y y y y y
```

Dimension 1 - called **rows** go down i.e. rowA, rowB, rowC …
Dimension 2 - called **columns** go across i.e. col1, col2 …

If I say, "… is seat 'A1' available, you go to (**rowA,col1**) and see the value = 'y'.

Moving closer to computers, if I say, "… what is the value in **seat(D,5)**?", you could answer, "… the value is '**n**'".

In programming, however, we do not refer to "seat(D,5)". Instead, we count how many rows down (which = 4), how many columns across (which = 5), and rather refer to **seat(4,5)**.

Let's leave it there.

10) IF Statements

Sometimes your program needs to choose one path or direction over another, based on the information being processed.

It only knows what the information is when the program starts running and this information might change each time you read a new record, or enter a new pupil. You need to be able to say:

IF I HAVE THIS SCENARIO
  THEN DO THE FOLLOWING: …………..

The program 'checks' if the scenario has been met. If met, it carries out the instruction. If not, it ignores the instruction.

You can also get the program to carry out some other instruction **if not** met:

IF I HAVE THIS SCENARIO
  DO THIS
OTHERWISE
  DO THAT

Example:

| READ RECORD FROM PUPIL-FILE |
| **IF** MATH MARK > 50 |
| THEN DISPLAY ON SCREEN 'PASS' |
| **ELSE** |
| DISPLAY ON SCREEN 'FAIL' |
| **END-IF** |

Note:

1. The END-IF, which starts and ends the IF statement.

2. The ELSE, which is not always required.

3. The layout (indentation) of the statement to make it more readable.

OR and AND statements

Sometimes we need to check if more than 1 condition is met. We use the 'AND' in our 'IF' statement to say that there are 2 things to check for i.e.

IF AGE IS A NUMBER **AND** NAME IS ALPHABETIC
THEN WRITE RECORD TO FILE
ENDIF

In the above example we will only 'WRITE RECORD TO FILE' if **both** 'AGE IS A NUMBER', AND 'NAME IS ALPHABETIC'.

Sometimes we only need for EITHER of 2 conditions to be met, in which case we use the 'OR'.

IF FIELD1 = 7 **OR** IF AGE > 30
THEN READ THE NEXT RECORD OF FILE1
ELSE
READ THE NEXT DELETE RECORD
ENDIF

Try following this logic for the above code:

- the program first checks if 'FIELD1 = 7'.

- If 'FIELD1 = 7', the program **doesn't bother** to check the 'OR' part i.e. 'IF AGE > 30', because the 1st condition is met before the 'OR'.

- It goes ahead and executes' READ NEXT RECORD …'.

- However, if 'FIELD1 **NOT = 7**', it checks the 2nd condition, i.e. 'IS AGE > 30'. If this is met, it will also execute the instruction 'READ THE NEXT RECORD OF FILE1'.

- IF neither condition is met, the program falls through to the 'OTHERWISE', and executes 'DELETE RECORD'.

11) Sub-Routines

Program Design

One of the rules of programming is that before you start typing up your program, you must 1st write it out on paper.

When building a house, (hopefully) the builders work to an original plan DESIGNED by an architect or building specialist. Imagine if there was no plan and they just started building and adding and changing as they went along without any plan. **Programmers are builders too, they build software.**

When building a program you need to design the flow, decide what to do when, make changes and adjustments on paper 1st, and then when ready, start typing it up.

Having said that, we need to also realize that there is good design and bad design.

Good design is a program that:
- is easy to read.
- that flows nicely.
- that does not repeat code unnecessarily.

The more time spent designing and planning on paper, the less time spent getting it right on the computer.

Sub-Routines help us to improve our design, so let's discuss these.

Sub-Routines / Sections/ Paragraphs

Sub-Routines, sections, paragraphs, forms, objects, are different names to describe the same thing. They are **blocks** or sections of programming code that are **grouped** together under a name. These lines of code in the 'block' have something in common and they are different or separate from other 'blocks of code', for better understanding.

Think of a text book. There are chapters in a text book, and there are paragraphs in each chapter. Certain stuff goes together because that's how it makes sense. We must also give each sub-routine its own heading. (Imagine a text book without headings at the start of each chapter). In some languages we also indicate the end of the routine, just like the examples below:

ADD-ROUTINE
ADD 1 TO …
ADD 2 TO …
MOVE …
READ …
END-ROUTINE
DISPLAY-ROUTINE
IF …
DISPLAY …
ELSE
DISPLAY …
ENDIF
END-ROUTINE

It is important to understand that any statements can be placed in a sub-routine. If we call a sub-routine ADD-ROUTINE, it does not mean that only 'ADD … ' statements can go in there. Just look at our examples above. We group lines of code into a 'named' block, which together perform a desired function.

Executing Sub-Routines

The beauty of having these sub-routines, among other things, is we can execute/call the same few lines of code from anywhere in the program, **without having to re-write** the code.

If we say:

```
EXECUTE ADD ROUTINE
```

The program will go to the 'ADD-ROUTINE', execute the lines of code and then return to the statement after the 'execute'. Looking at the code below:

PROGRAM START
MOVE ABC TO …
EXECUTE DISPLAY-ROUTINE
MOVE XYZ …
EXECUTE ADD-ROUTINE
EXECUTE DISPLAY-ROUTINE
DISPLAY-ROUTINE
IF …
DISPLAY …
ELSE
DISPLAY …
ENDIF
END-ROUTINE
ADD-ROUTINE
ADD 1 TO …
ADD 2 TO …
MOVE …
READ …
END-ROUTINE

- we start with 'MOVE ABC TO …'.

- we then execute the 'DISPLAY-ROUTINE', so drop down to the 'IF …' in the 'DISPLAY-ROUTINE' block, and process each line until the END-ROUTINE.

- we then jump back up to the 'MOVE XYZ …'.

- we then execute the 'ADD-ROUTINE', so drop down to the 'ADD 1 TO …' in the 'ADD-ROUTINE' block, and process each line until the END-ROUTINE.

- we then execute the 'DISPLAY-ROUTINE' **again**, so drop down to the 'IF …' again, and so on.

- NO REPETITION OF CODE
- NICE FLOW
- EASY TO READ
- GOOD DESIGN

12) Calling other Programs

It is possible to be in one program and make a 'call' to another program. We then **branch off** to the 'called' program, execute the 'called' program, then return to where we left off in the 'calling' program.

PROGRAM NAME: PROG A
…
MOVE XYZ …
CALL 'PROG B'
ADD 5 TO …
…

1. We start off in program *PROG A* (the calling program).
2. Process until line *CALL 'PROG B'*.
3. *Branch of to 'PROG B' (the called program)*.
4. Execute all the code in 'PROG B'.
5. Return to the next statement in 'PROG A' 'ADD 5 TO …'.

This is **similar** to **sub-routines**, although here we are leaving our program and branching off to a completely different program, as oppose to a sub-routine in the same program.

Can you think of a reason we might want to do this?

Imagine the same few lines of code are needed in 1000 different programs. Is it 'good design' to write the same few lines of code 1000 times? That would be silly. We rather place those lines in their own program, and issue a 'call' to that program wherever the code is needed.

Passing Parameters

Let's take it up a notch.

It is possible to call a program and at the same time, pass information into that program. This information we pass is then used in the 'called' program.

CALL 'PROG B' **PASSING** FIELD1

The above statement is actually saying, "Call 'PROG B' and pass into it the data in FIELD1".

We need to be set up in the 'called' program ('PROG B') to be able to accept this data.

PROGRAM NAME: PROG B **USING** FIELD1

The above statement is the 1st line of PROGRAM 'PROG B'. It says, "I am a called program and I will use the contents of FIELD1 passed to me".

Yip, you guessed it. If the value of FIELD1 now changes in the 'called' program (PROG B), when we return to the 'calling' program (PROG A), we pass back the changed value.

Let's see an example.

PROGRAM NAME: **PROG A**
MOVE 1 TO FIELD1
CALL 'PROG B' PASSING FIELD1
DISPLAY FIELD1

- 'PROG A' is the 'calling' program.
- When it calls 'PROG B', it also passes the field FIELD1 (with the value of '1') into 'PROG B'.

PROGRAM NAME: **PROG B USING FIELD1**
DISPLAY FIELD1
ADD 1 TO FIELD1

- 'PROG B' is the 'called' program.
- The 'DISPLAY' would display '1', because that was the value passed through.
- The next statement would make FIELD1 = 2 (ADD 1 TO FIELD1).
- The program would then return to 'PROG A', to the statement after the 'CALL' (DISPLAY FIELD1).
- The 'DISPLAY' in 'PROG A' would now display '2', as this was the value passed back from 'PROG B'.

13) Databases

Throughout the text, we have seen the term 'File/Table'. It is time to split the 'File' from the 'Table'.

Batch vs Real Time Processing

The origin of computers gave us the ability to process huge amounts of data at once. We could read through and process thousands upon thousands of records. This 'bulk' processing of files, i.e. starting at the beginning of the file, processing each record, until the end of the file is reached, is called **Batch Processing**. We usually set these programs off, go make some coffee and come back once all the processing is done.

With the evolution of computers (and programmers), we then decided we had to be able to work with 1 particular record on demand.

For example, you phone the bank to say your credit card is lost and they must stop the card. They ask you a bunch of questions and then go and fetch (read) your particular details off the computer files, and do what needs to be done. We call this **Real Time** or **On-line** processing. Can you see how in 'real time' we need to work with one record on demand at any moment in time, whereas 'batch processing' described above worked through a huge file of records one by one.

Let's give another example of both:

Batch Processing – reading through our Pupil File and printing a report card for each student.

Real Time – accessing the Teacher Table and changing the surname of Miss. Jiles to Mrs. Peter's.

With Real Time processing, came the need for our files to be better organized. We needed to be able to quickly fetch the record we require, and make the change. This was the catalyst for **databases**.

My Database Recipe.

- *take a bunch of files (like the ones we have been using).*
- *throw in a tool to control and manage these files.*
- *throw in indexes (like the ones in books) to sort these files.*
- *throw in special commands to access the data in the files.*
- *mix this all up and collectively you have a database.*

It is important to understand that a database is just a collection of files. These files are now called **TABLES**, and like other files, contain records and fields. With these tables we will read, write to, and change data, but using a slightly different method.

As mentioned above, special commands were developed to help access these tables. These commands are pretty similar in all languages and based on 1 particular language called 'Structured Query Language' or SQL. Let's see some examples.

1. When we want to get a record from a table we could say:

```
SELECT *
FROM PUPIL TABLE
WHERE NAME = 'SMITH'.
```

This is known as a **QUERY** of a table. We are saying:

- select all the fields of the record
- from the *PUPIL TABLE* (file in database)
- where the *Name = 'Smith'*

Note the '.' at the end of each QUERY. This helps to tell us where the query ends.

```
SELECT NAME,ADDRESS
FROM PUPIL TABLE
WHERE NAME = 'SMITH'.
```

- we can also select **certain** fields from the record, as oppose to each field in the record, to reduce processing time like above.
- the fields *NAME* and *ADDRESS* were read only.

2. When we wish to update a particular record:

```
UPDATE PUPIL TABLE
SET MATH MARK = 80%
WHERE NAME = "VINNIE VIKI".
```

- with the **UPDATE** you can specify which field you wish to change in the record, in this case we only changed the *MATH MARK*.

3. When we wish to delete a record from a table:

```
DELETE PUPIL TABLE
WHERE NAME = "DANNY SMITH".
```

- the **DELETE** will delete the entire record.

4. When we wish to Insert a record into the table:

```
INSERT INTO PUPIL TABLE
NAME,MATH MARK, ENGLISH MARK
    VALUES
        WS-NAME, WS-MATH, WS-ENGLISH.
```

You may need to read the INSERT a few times over, but this is the best way to get it.

INSERT a record into *PUPIL TABLE* using the following values:

- Get the value of Table field *'NAME'* from *'WS_NAME'*.
- Get the value of Table field *'MATH MARK'* from *'WS-MATH MARK'*.
- Get the value of Table field *'ENGLISH MARK'* from *'WS-ENGLISH MARK'*.

So replacing flat files with tables, we have replaced:

READ with **SELECT**
WRITE with **INSERT**
REWRITE with **UPDATE**

Defining Tables

Tables are described and defined to the database **before** the programs make use of them. The designer will specify which **fields** are needed for each **record**.

So our database manager would let us define the following:

DATABASE NAME: SCHOOL DATA
TABLE1 NAME: TEACHER TABLE
TABLE2 NAME: PUPIL TABLE
TABLE3 NAME: SPORTS RESULTS

TABLE1: TEACHER TABLE
FIELD1: NAME 20 bytes Alphanumeric
FIELD2: ADDRESS 50 bytes Alphanumeric
FIELD3: CLASS   3 bytes Numeric
FIELD4: SALARY 9 bytes Numeric
TABLE2: PUPIL TABLE
.
.
.

We therefore **do not** need to define the layout in our programs like we did for files.

Now using tables, we just specify the table name in the QUERY and let the computer brain do the rest.

PROGRAM START
SELECT NAME,ADDRESS FROM TEACHER TABLE WHERE ...

Sample Program

Let's build something using databases. Assume we have already created a database for the school and we now want a program to help manage the teachers.

Our program will give the user the option to VIEW, ADD, CHANGE or DELETE teachers (comments will be on the right).

TEMPORARY STORAGE	*no files defined as using tables*
TS-ACTION	1 byte, Numeric
TS-NAME	20 bytes, Alphanumeric
TS-ADDRESS	50 bytes, Alphanumeric
TS-SALARY	9 bytes, Numeric
TS-CLASS	3 bytes, Numeric
PROGRAM START	
DISPLAY "ENTER 1 TO VIEW TEACHER	
ENTER 2 TO ADD TEACHER	
ENTER 3 TO DELETE TEACHER"	
ENTER 4 TO CHANGE TEACHER	
PUT INTO TS-ACTION	*TS-ACTION = 1,2,3 or 4*
IF ACTION = 1	*Execute Different Routines*
EXECUTE 'DISPLAY-TEACHER'	
ELSEIF ACTION = 2	
EXECUTE 'ADD-TEACHER'	
ELSEIF ACTION = 3	
EXECUTE 'DELETE-TEACHER'	
ELSEIF ACTION = 4	
EXECUTE 'CHANGE-TEACHER'	
ENDIF	
PROGRAM-END	
DISPLAY-TEACHER ROUTINE	
DISPLAY 'ENTER TEACHER NAME'	*enter teacher to display*
PUT INTO WS-NAME	*send from keyboard to temp*
SELECT *	*fetch the teacher from tab*
FROM TEACHER-TABLE	
WHERE NAME = WS-NAME	
DISPLAY TEACHER-TABLE-NAME	*display selected record*
TEACHER-TABLE-ADDRESS	
TEACHER-TABLE-SALARY	
TEACHER-TABLE-CLASS	
END-ROUTINE	
ADD-TEACHER ROUTINE	
DISPLAY 'ENTER TEACHER NAME	*tell user what to enter*
ENTER ADDRESS	
ENTER SALARY	
ENTER CLASS'	
PUT INTO WS-NAME	*send data from keyboard*
PUT INTO WS-ADDRES	
PUT INTO WS-SALARY	
PUT INTO WS-CLASS	
INSERT INTO TEACHER-TABLE	*write data to table*
NAME,ADDRESS,SALARY,CLASS	
VALUES	
WS-NAME,WS-ADDRESS,WS-SALARY,WS-CLASS	
END-ROUTINE	
CHANGE-TEACHER ROUTINE	
DISPLAY 'ENTER TEACHER TO CHANGE'	
PUT INTO WS-NAME	

```
SELECT *                              fetch the teacher data
   FROM TEACHER-TABLE
     WHERE NAME = WS-NAME
DISPLAY TEACHER-TABLE-NAME            display selected record
        TEACHER-TABLE-ADDRESS
        TEACHER-TABLE-SALARY
        TEACHER-TABLE-CLASS
PUT INTO WS-NAME                      send from keyboard to temp
PUT INTO WS-ADDRES
```

```
PUT INTO WS-SALARY

PUT INTO WS-CLASS
UPDATE TEACHER-TABLE                  update record with new data
   SET NAME,ADDRESS,SALARY,CLASS
      VALUES
   WS-NAME,WS-ADDRESS,WS-SALARY,WS-CLASS
```
END-ROUTINE

DELETE-TEACHER ROUTINE
```
DISPLAY 'ENTER TEACHER TO DELETE'
PUT INTO WS-NAME
DELETE *                             delete the teacher entered
   FROM TEACHER-TABLE
     WHERE NAME = WS-NAME
```
END-ROUTINE

14) Sorting data

We have discussed storing data in files and databases tables. If we look a little deeper at the data, we will soon realize that often, we need to have the data sorted in a certain sequence.

E.g. if we are printing a list of pupils, surely we would want the output to be listed alphabetically …

1. Adams, John   55 4th Ave
2. Brown, Steve   23 3rd St
3. Green, Mary   12 2nd Ave
4. Harri, Jimmy   10 5th St
5. Jones, Will   14 3rd Ave
6. …

We always need to ask, where is the source of our data (i.e. file, database, table) and in what sequence is this data stored. Let's look at a couple of scenarios.

Sorting Files

If the above data is stored in a file, we need to ask what order was the file sorted in originally? We usually get the following situations:

- the file is already sorted in the sequence you need it.

- the file is not sorted at all.

- the file is sorted in, say, 'Telephone number' sequence, and we need it in 'Name' sequence.

If the file is already sorted in the sequence you need, no problem – just go ahead and 'do what ya gotta do'.

If the file does need to be sorted in a particular sequence there are various methods to do this. For now, it is good enough to know that the following statement is possible:

```
SORT FILE (FILENAME) BY FIELD/S e.g.
```

```
SORT PUPIL FILE BY NAME
```

Sorting Database Tables

Databases work differently. They are designed to allow you to keep them sorted on a certain 'field' all the time. As you add a new record, it is slotted in the correct place automatically.

The field/s that the database table is sorted on is called the 'key' field/s. You can choose the key/s when you set up the table.

```
DATABASE NAME: SCHOOL DATA

TABLE1 NAME: TEACHER TABLE
KEY: NAME     20 bytes Alphanumeric
     ADDRESS  50 bytes Alphanumeric
     CLASS     3 bytes Numeric
     SALARY    9 bytes Numeric

TABLE2: PUPIL TABLE
```

The above database table has all the records sorted in 'NAME' sequence, as 'NAME' is key field. The table would look like this:

Adams, Mr. 45 3rd Ave Grade 1 $3000
Brown, Mrs.16 4th Ave Grade 2 $2000
Jones, Mr. 15 3rd Ave Grade 4 $1000
...

If you wanted to display each record, it would come out in the 'key' sequence stored above.

```
SELECT * from TEACHER-TABLE
   Display data
ENDSELECT
```

ORDER BY

If however, you desire the data to be read in a different sequence to the 'key' sequence, you can use the **'ORDER BY'**, in the **SELECT** statement. This way, you can have the data read in **any** order you choose (as below):

```
SELECT * from TEACHER-TABLE ORDER BY SALARY
   Display data
ENDSELECT
```

The above table is now being accessed in order of 'SALARY'. If displayed, the data would look as follows:

Jones, Mr. 15 3rd Ave Grade 4 **$1000**
Brown, Mrs.16 4th Ave Grade 2 **$2000**
Adams, Mr. 45 3rd Ave Grade 1 **$3000**

15) Web Design & Internet Programming

People often confuse 'web design' with 'internet programming'. I thought I'd conclude *BOOK I* with a brief comparison of the 2 disciplines.

To explain the difference (and similarities), let's imagine we are looking at a web page, say a cool movie site.

The amazing images you see, and scroll bars, and links and information and colors and … and … and …, that is presented to you on the screen is called the **'*look and feel*'**. This 'look and feel', which requires a large amount of creativity, is developed by the **'web designer'**.

Now, let's say the site also has a competition to win a cell phone. In order to win, you must enter information *(name, address, email)*. Once the information is type in on the form, and you hit 'ENTER', the data is pushed through into a program where it is inserted into a database. This part is done by the 'internet programmer'.

Please note there is a fine line between them. In fact the form, transporting the data can be done by web designers. The minute we start using this data, things become less 'creative' and start leaning toward the 'programming' side.

Some folks can do both, but usually they are split into 2 roles. Having said that, the tool used to present or convert all that you see on the browser page (which is not for this course) is also a language, and so theoretically, 'web designers' are programmers too.

GOOD LUCK AND ENJOY!!

BOOK II

As mentioned above, BOOK II delves deeper into the topics discussed above. Some of the ideas might get a bit tricky, so I recommend re-reading these sections if you get stuck.

If you found 'BOOK I' difficult, I suggest you skip the following technical chapters and read from Chapter 23 onward, for some easier reading and some interesting ideas on the world of programming.

16) Moving Data across Different Field Types

We covered field 'types' in Book I. Now let's dig a little deeper and discuss movements between these fields.

One must be very careful when moving data across different field types.

Alphabetic to Alphanumeric

Alphabetic fields to Alphanumeric fields is no problem as Alphanumeric fields can store any characters.

Alphanumeric to Alphabetic

Alphanumeric fields to Alphabetic fields are problematic if the characters are not 'a-z', 'A-Z', or the ' ' (space). Moving **'!?/'** to an alphabetic field will cause the program to crash.

Numeric to Alphabetic

Numeric fields to Alphabetic fields will definitely crash the program.

Numeric to Alphanumeric

Numeric fields to Alphanumeric fields will not crash, although this move may provide problematic results:

   o the sign is not carried over which is OK if your numeric value is +ve, but if it is -ve, the sign is lost.

   o if your field lengths are the same, no problem but if they are not you will either lose digits, or have spaces at the end.

When moving data from *FIELD1* to *FIELD2*, the rules are always governed by the **receiving** field i.e. *FIELD2*. Since we are moving to an Alphanumeric, we fill the bytes from **left to right**:

o If you move **123** (Numeric, 3 bytes) to an (Alphanumeric, 2 byte) field your receiving field will contain **'12'**. Note how the 3 is lost.

o If you move 123 (Numeric, 3 bytes) to an (Alphanumeric, 5 bytes) field, the receiving field will contain '123'. Note the trailing 2 spaces after the 3.

Alphanumeric to Numeric

Alphanumeric fields other than numbers will definitely crash.

Alphanumeric fields that contain numbers will generally be OK but again, you may get undesirable results if the field lengths are different.

When we move data to a Numeric field, we fill the bytes from **right to left.**

o If you move **'123'** (Alphanumeric, 3 bytes) to a (Numeric, 2 byte) field your receiving field will contain **23**. Note how the 1 is lost.

o If you move **'123'** (Alphanumeric, 3 byte) to a (Numeric, 5 byte) your receiving field will contain **00123**.

Having said all of this, these rules are the norm but I definitely would not assume they are the same for every language. The message to take out of this chapter is to be very careful when moving data across different field types.

Should the occasion arise, I strongly urge you to test your code by displaying the results of the receiving field with test data. This way you will establish the exact rules for that particular language.

17) Numeric Fields Continued

The Sign

When using numeric fields, you need to cater for a **'-ve'** value. Let's look at 3 numeric fields used in some arithmetic.

FieldA (1 byte, numeric, value=2)
FieldB (1 byte, numeric, value=3)
FIELDC (1 byte, numeric, **Signed**)

Example 1.   FieldC = FieldA - FieldB
                 = 3 - 2
                 = 1

Example 2.   FieldC = FieldB - FieldA
                 = 2 - 3
                 = -1

How did we cater for the -1?

In some languages, you **need to specify** that a field must be able to store '-ve' values, otherwise the sign is lost, hence the **'Signed'** clause in the above definition of FieldC.

If you defined the field as: FieldC (1 byte, numeric), then

FieldC = FieldB - FieldA
= 2 - 3
= **1** (as you have not catered for the sign)

Some languages have different formats of numeric fields and some of these cater for the '-ve' by default. If this is the case, you will need to know which type of numeric field to use, otherwise, don't forget to specify your sign.

Decimal Values

In all languages you will need to specifically cater for

decimal places if your values contain them i.e. **9999.99**. Each language will have its own way of doing this but in general you will ask:

how many digits and how many decimals included?

999.99   = 5 digits (in total), with 2 decimals
9999.999   = 7 digits, 3 decimals

to define these fields, you will **generally** say something like:

FIELDA   **5 bytes, numeric, 2 decimals**

Remember each digit = 1 byte, so:
'3 bytes, 2 decimals' would be able to store:

9.99 or 1.23 or 5.67.

FIELDB   **5 bytes, numeric, 1 decimal** - would be able to store:

1234.5 or 6789.1

Please note that the **decimal point** does **not** take up a byte at all. The computer assigns a field pointer to where the decimal point sits, so when counting bytes, do not include the decimal point.

Packed Fields

This little section is bit more complicated, so just try to get the idea.

We stated above that: **each digit = 1 byte**. This is the **default** way we store numbers, so

FIELDA   **Numeric, 3 bytes, value = 123** - has 123 stored in 3 bytes.

The way we actually store the number is by splitting each byte in half (4 bits|4 bits), and assigning each digit to the 2nd 4 bits.

Byte 1	Byte 2	Byte 3
----|----	----|----	----|----
1	2	3

The value assigned to the 1ˢᵗ 4 digits of each byte is actually hexadecimal 'F', so in theory the 3 bytes actually contain: **F1F2F3**.

Byte 1	Byte 2	Byte 3
----|----	----|----	----|----
F 1	F 2	F 3

(Not to worry, you won't walk around saying your data has F1F2F3 in it, but you will get to scrutinize bytes and you will recognize that F1F2F3 is '123'.)

Now to save millions of bytes in memory, it is possible to **replace** the Hexadecimal 'F' with a digit and **PACK** the digits together (except for the last 'F').

Byte 1	Byte 2
----|----	----|----
1 2	3 F

This is called a packed field. Note how by packing the digits, we saved 1 byte. If you had a file of 30 million records, with a couple of these fields, you have saved a couple million bytes.

To define 'packed' numeric fields, you would either use a format that is specifically for packed data or you would have to specify that the field is packed i.e.

```
FIELDB Numeric, 3 digits, Packed.
```

18) How to Unload Tables (Arrays)

Unloading 1 dimensional tables

In BOOK I, we covered the topic of tables (arrays). Let's look at unloading both 1 and 2 dimensional tables onto a printout. (Note we are not dealing here with a Database table, but an array of data, repeated many times)

Let's first define an array set up to hold pupil information in a class.

Pupil Info	Occurs 30 times
pupil-name	30 bytes, alphanumeric
pupil-age	3 bytes, numeric

Remember, this has defined space for 30 pupils, each pupil having a 'Name' and an 'Age'.

Let's use a field in temporary storage to help, and let's define our print line:

Count	2 bytes, numeric
Printline.	
Printline-name	30 bytes, alphanumeric
Printline-age.	3 bytes, numeric

Now let's print out every pupil, by looping through the table:

```
Set count = 1
DO until count > 30
    Move pupil-name(count) to printline-name
    Move pupil-age(count) to printline-age
    Write out printline
    Add 1 to count
ENDDO
```

We could expect to see something like this on the printout:

Mary Jane   *009*
Jimmy Smith   *008*
Johnny Jones   *010*
. . .

Looking at this printout, you also get a feel for what the table looks like, but remember, in storage the bytes are stacked together.

Let's now take it up a notch and do the same for 2 dimensional tables.

Unloading 2 dimensional tables

We have already defined a table of pupils in a class. Now what if we said there were 5 different classes, each of 30 pupils?

As we have discussed, there is no need to write the Pupil Table out 5 times. We would rather build a 2 dimensional table.

The 1st dimension, storing the 'class' information, and the 2nd dimension, storing the 'pupil' information (per class).

Note below, how the 'pupil-info Occurs 30', is treated just like another field, belonging to the Class-info table, i.e. it is a table, within a table.

Class info Occurs 5 times	
Class-name	30 bytes, alphanumeric
Teacher-name	30 bytes, alphanumeric
Pupil-Info Occurs 30 times	
Pupil-name	30 bytes, alphanumeric
Pupil-age	3 bytes, numeric

We would need 2 counters now, one for 'class' and one for 'pupil', and we would need to define an extra 'printline' for the 'class' details:

Class-count	2 bytes, numeric
Pupil-count.	2 bytes, numeric
Pupil-printline.	
Pupil-printline-name	30 bytes, alphanumeric
Pupil-printline-age.	3 bytes, numeric
Class-printline.	
Class-printline-name	30 bytes, alphanumeric
Class-printline-teacher	30 bytes, alphanumeric

```
Set class-count = 1

DO until class-count > 5 (go through the 5 classes)

   Move class-name(class-count) to class-printline-name
   Move teacher-name(class-count) to class-printline-teacher
   Write out class-printline

   Set pupil-count = 1

   DO until pupil-count > 30 (then process the 30 pupils in each class)

      Move pupil-name (class-count, pupil-count) to printline-name
      Move pupil-age (class-count, pupil-count) to printline-age
      Write out pupil-printline
      Add 1 to pupil-count

   ENDDO

   Add 1 to class-count

ENDDO
```

Your printout might look something like this:

Grade 3.   Mr. Jones

      Mary Jane   009
      Jimmy Smith   008
      Johnny Jones   010
                ;;;

Grade 4.   Mrs. Smith

      Jack Long   011
      Sally Short   011
      Danny King   011
                ;;;

… and so on.

19) Matching and Merging Files

Matching files

We often get a situation where there are 2 (or more) files containing **different information** that need to be linked together to combine the data.

When I say "*linked together*", I mean take some (or all) of the fields of a record from File 1. and combine these with some (or all) of the fields of a record in File 2.

Then, do something with these combined fields, like create a new record and print it out.

We wouldn't just **link** any records from the 2 files. We would **match** the records 1st that have something in common like 'Name' or 'Account Number' or 'Registration Number'.

The quickest way to grasp this is to look at an example. Let's look at 2 files:

Class-data-file	
class	10 bytes, alpha
teacher	30 bytes, alpha

Teacher-data-file	
name	30 bytes, alpha
address	30 bytes, alpha

We have been told that the common field in the above 2 files is the teacher's name (i.e. field 'teacher' in the 'Class-data-file' and 'name' in the 'Teacher-data-file').

Let's say the task at hand is to read through the files and write out the **class name**, the **teacher's name** and the **teacher's address**. Looking at the files, can you see we need to use both files as the **teacher's address** is only found on the **'Teacher-data-file'**? We would match these files.

Let's build some test data:

Class-data-file		*Teacher-data-file*		
Grade 1	Mr Smith	Mr Smith	6 9th Rd...	
Grade 2	Mr Jones	Mr Jones	8 3rd Rd...	
Grade 3	Ms Blue	Ms Blue	5 4th St...	
Grade 4	Ms Green	Ms Green	6 7th St...	

After matching the 2 files and printing the output, we would get something like this:

Grade 1	Mr Smith	6 9th Rd...
Grade 2	Mr Jones	8 3rd Rd...
Grade 3	Ms Blue	5 4th St...
Grade 4	Ms Green	6 7th St...

To match the right records, in the correct order, a methodology called **"low-key processing"** is used, which we will leave for another chapter.

Merging files

Merging files is a similar concept as above, but in this case, the 2 (or more files) contain **identical fields in the records**, and the goal is to combine all the data.

Imagine a retail store has sales data for each day of the week (Mon to Fri). On Saturday, a program runs that combines the files for each day. Let's see what the files might look like:

Mon-sales-file	
Product	7 bytes, alpha
Total-sold	4 bytes, numeric

Tue-sales-file	
Product	7 bytes, alpha
Total-sold	4 bytes, numeric

Wed-sales-file	
Product	7 bytes, alpha
Total-sold	4 bytes, numeric

(... and so on for Thu, Fri)

Let's look at test data: each file stores a **product** and **no. of sales** per day.

Mon-sales-file		*Tue-sales-file*		*Wed-sales-file*	
Boots	1000	Boots	2000	Boots	3000
Caps	500	Caps	550	Caps	570
Denims	600	Denims	660	Denims	690
Hats	700	Hats	730	Hats	790

After **merging** the 3 files into 1, we could expect:

Boots	1000
Boots	2000
Boots	3000
Caps	500
Caps	550
Caps	570
Denims	600
Denims	660
Denims	690
Hats	700
Hats	730
Hats	790

(When 'merging' files, we will also use "low-key processing" to get the correct records in the right sequence, which will be discussed in another chapter.)

20) Low-Key Processing

We previously discussed the concept of 'matching' and 'merging' files. We said the methodology used to process the correct records in the correct order is called 'low-key processing'. Let's look at this 'low-key processing' a little closer.

All programming tools required for 'low-key processing' have been covered in BOOK I.

What does the 'lower key' mean? Well if you have the word: 'apple' and the word: 'banana', the 'a' from 'apple' comes **before** the 'b' from 'banana', and so the *lower key* is 'apple'.

If you are comparing numbers, the number '100' comes before the number '200', and so the lower key is '100'. Another way to say it that 'apple' is smaller than 'banana' and hence the lower key.

The word 'key' is used because it is a 'key' field, used to determine the order of records in the file.

This concept is used when 'matching' and 'merging' files (as described above) to ensure the data comes out in the right order. To demonstrate this, I will work with 2 files, but remember that there is no limit to the number of files that can be used.

Let's use our *'sales files'* again …

Mon-sales-file	
Product	7 bytes, alpha
Total-sold	4 bytes, numeric

Tue-sales-file	
Product	7 bytes, alpha
Total-sold	4 bytes, numeric

Mon-sales-file		Tue-sales-file	
Caps	500	Boots	2000
Denims	600	Caps	550
Hats	700	Hats	730
		Jackets	600

(Note how 'Tue-sales-file' did not sell *Denims* but did sell *Jackets,* and 'Mon-sales-file' did not sell *Boots*)

Our task is to *combine* the files, outputting *all the sales in alphabetical order.*

Let's first take a peek at what our output should look like at the end to get an idea of what we are aiming at:

The output must be sorted in 'product' order i.e.

Boots	2000	(from Tue-)
Caps	500	(from Mon-)
Caps	550	(from Tue-)
Denims	600	(from Mon-)
Hats	700	(from Mon-)
Hats	730	(from Tue-)
Jackets	600	(from Mon-)

If I said the output should be in the order of 'Total Sold', can you see that the output would look like this? :

Caps	500	(from Mon-)
Caps	550	(from Tue-)
Denims	600	(from Mon-)
Jackets	600	(from Mon-)
Hats	700	(from Mon-)
Hats	730	(from Tue-)
Boots	2000	(from Tue-)

As discussed in BOOK I, we always draw the design on paper first. If you are attempting 'low-key processing' without a design on paper you are wasting your time.

Please bear in mind that there are a few variations of 'low-key processing' depending on the contents of the files, but the concept is essentially the same across all. We will discuss the simplest form in order to grasp the idea.

Are the files sorted?

Looking at the 2 files, you can see that they are **sorted** in alphabetical order of 'Product'. This is **absolutely essential**. If your files are not sorted in the correct order, your processing will have to start off by doing 'sorts' on each file.

When we refer to 'low-key processing', the **'key'** is the *field/s* on which the files have been sorted, in our case *'Product'*.

First we create a field in temporary storage called *'low-key'*, which we make **similar to the key field** (in our case Product).

Low-key 7 bytes, alpha

The basic process we follow is:

- by **reading both files** one by one, always keep track of which file's key *(product in our case)* has the **lowest** value. That way we keep things in order, i.e., Boots 1st, then Caps, then Denims, then Hats …

- only work with records if their key is the **lowest** value.

We'll start with a broad design and then drill down: **(you will need to focus here, and it may take a few reads but do yourself a favor and get this behind you)**. Undoubtedly the best and only way to grasp this is to actually take the test data and work it through the design.

Try to follow the design below:

```
READ FILE1
READ FILE2

DO UNTIL both files have had all records read

   PERFORM LOW-KEY (find the lowest key from both files)

   DO UNTIL File1-key NOT EQUAL to low-key value
      PROCESS File1 records
   ENDDO

   DO UNTIL File2-key NOT EQUAL to low-key value
      PROCESS File2 records
   ENDDO

ENDDO
```

Now let's explore the code a little more, and the order it is executed:

```
Read record from Mon-sales-file (1)
Read record from Tue-sales-file (2)

Do the following, until both Mon-sales-file and Tue-sales-file have read all
records (3)

   Perform Find-Low-key (branch off to section 'Find-low-key' and then return) (4)

   Do the following until value in 'product' of Mon-sales record is not equal to
   value in 'low-key' (10)


      Display product of  Mon-sales record (11)
      Display total-sold of  Mon-sales record (12)
      Read next record of Mon-sales-file (13)

   Enddo (14)

   Do the following until value in 'product' of Tue-sales record is not equal to
   value in 'low-key' (15)


      Display product of  Tue-sales record (16)
      Display total-sold of  Tue-sales record (17)
      Read next record of Tue-sales-file (18)

   Enddo (19)

Enddo (20)
```

FIND-LOW-KEY SECTION
If value in 'product' of Mon-sales-file is < **value** in 'product' of Tue-sales-file **(5)**
Move 'product' of Mon-sales-file to 'low-key' **(6)**
Else (otherwise) **(7)**
Move 'product' of Tue-sales-file to 'low-key' **(8)**
End-if (9)

Following the order of executed code above, let's see what the **key values** are at each line of code:

Mon-sales-file
Caps	500
Denims	600
Hats	700

Tue-sales-file
Boots	2000
Caps	550
Hats	730
Jackets	600

Line No	Product (Mon)	Product (Tue)	Low-key
1.	**Caps**	(empty)	(empty)
2.	Caps	**Boots**	(empty)
3.	Caps	Boots	(empty)
4.	Caps	Boots	(empty)
5.	Caps	Boots	(empty)
7.	Caps	Boots	(empty)
8.	Caps	Boots	**Boots**
9.	Caps	Boots	Boots
10.	Caps	Boots	Boots
14.	Caps	Boots	Boots
15.	Caps	Boots	Boots
16.	Caps	Boots	Boots
17.	Caps	Boots	Boots
18.	Caps	**Caps**	Boots
15.	Caps	Caps	Boots
19.	Caps	Caps	Boots
3.	Caps	Caps	Boots
4.	Caps	Caps	Boots
5.	Caps	Caps	Boots
7.	Caps	Caps	Boots
8.	Caps	Caps	**Caps**
9.	Caps	Caps	Caps
10.	Caps	Caps	Caps
11.	Caps	Caps	Caps
12.	Caps	Caps	Caps
13.	**Denims**	Caps	Caps

Line No	Product (Mon)	Product (Tue)	Low-key
10.	Denims	Caps	Caps
14.	Denims	Caps	Caps
15.	Denims	Caps	Caps
16.	Denims	Caps	Caps
17.	Denims	Caps	Caps
18.	Denims	**Hats**	Caps
15.	Denims	Hats	Caps
19.	Denims	Hats	Caps
3.	Denims	Hats	Caps
4.	Denims	Hats	Caps
5.	Denims	Hats	Caps
6.	Denims	Hats	***Denims***
9.	Denims	Hats	Denims
10.	Denims	Hats	Denims

Try continuing yourself…

21) Object Oriented (OO) Programming

This book would be incomplete without mentioning Object Oriented ('OO') programming.

OO programming is a **methodology** or **approach** to programming. It is not a new concept, although it is becoming very popular and being adopted by many programming languages. It is also not the easiest concept to grasp and so I will try to keep it as simple as possible. Note that to master Object Oriented programming takes a great deal of practice, and it is definitely not something that is expected from beginners.

Objects

As the name suggests, the basic principle of 'OO' programming is dealing with **'objects'**. What is an 'object'?

*If your program had to keep records of 'books' in a library, **each** 'book' would be an 'object' of all the 'books'.*

*If your program was used to help sell 'cars', **each** 'car' would be an 'object' of all the 'cars'.*

*If your program was used to keep information on 'customers', **each** 'customer' would be an 'object' of all the 'customers'.*

Attributes

As you can imagine, each 'object', could have a number of fields to describe it:

Book 'object'
- Title
- Author
- Publisher

Car 'object'
- Make
- Color
- Price

The fields described above are also known as **ATTRIBUTES**.

Now in our program, when dealing with an 'object', we will obviously be doing something with that 'object'.

We can say we have **ACTIONS** on an 'object'. Some examples:

- Calculate car price
- Add car to database
- Change car in database
- List car spare parts

These **actions** are actual 'sections' in the program. So you have a 'Calculate car price' section and an 'Add car to database' section. These sections are lines no different to what we have described in previous chapters. Some languages refer to these sections of code as **'methods'**.

We discussed above the concept of calling a 'program' from within another program and passing 'fields' forward and backward.

The same can be done with 'methods'. We can call these methods from any program, and once we are in the method, we can then use the 'attributes' as fields.

Let us dig a little deeper.

So, we have ATTRIBUTES + ACTIONS. In fact the combination of the two make up what is known as a **'CLASS'**.

CLASS = ATTRIBUTES + ACTIONS.

The **'cars' class** = 'car' attributes + 'car' actions … or we can say the **'customer' class** which is made up of 'customer' attributes + 'customer' actions.

In a program, each class could be used a number of times. Each time we use the class, we use a different **object** of that class. We apply the possible 'actions' belonging to that class, using the possible 'attributes'.

In programming we define the class, and say
- What are the attributes
- What are the methods (actions).

CLASS DEFINITION
CLASS NAME = 'CAR'
ATTRIBUTES
- Make
- Model
- Color
- Price
METHODS
- Add car to database
- Calculate Price
- Change details
- List spare parts

Then we would have to define each method by typing out the code to perform the desired action i.e.

Method: Add car to database
...
Move ...
Add ...
Insert into database ...
Method: Calculate Price
... and so on

Let us look at how this could be used.

Perhaps we need a new program that captures cars into a database. We could use the method 'Add car to database' in the above class to do this.

PROGRAM A
Enter Make: _____
Enter Model: _____
Enter Color: _____
CALL **class** 'CARS' -> **action**: Add car to database
USING **attributes**: Make, Model, Color

Each time we use the above 'method', we are creating a new **'object'** of the 'car' class. Remember, we call the defined 'method', and execute the defined code belonging to that method.

Continuing with our example, now we decide we want a new program that does a bunch of stuff, and amongst this stuff, we need to know the price of a car.

"Aha!", we remember we have this 'car class', which amongst other things, has a module that can calculate a price.

This time we call the method to get a value back:

PROGRAM B
…
CALL class 'CARS' -> **action: calculate price**
USING attribute: Make, Model
GETTING BACK attribute: **Price**

I hope I have given you a basic understanding of using objects. To be perfectly honest, my understanding of OO programming is not as good as I would like it to be. I know that for me to get there, I need to put my head down and work at it.

22) Printing Files

Somewhere along the line in your programming career you are going to be required to build reports that will be printed onto paper.

Some will be small and simple, others long and complex. There are a few main issues to discuss:

Print Files

Generally speaking, when printing, we are writing out records to an **Output File**. We do this exactly the same way we have discussed writing to 'Output files' in Book I. Each record contains the line of data that we are going to print. This 'Output file' is then **spooled** (sent) to the printer.

This is done by using a combination of our 'Output file', the 'operating system' (also discussed Book I) and specialized programs that actually execute on the printer.

New Pages

When printing, the computer and printer do not know how many lines have printed on a page, or when it is time to jump to a new page.

Therefore, the program needs to count how many records have been written (lines printed) and after approximately 50 lines (depending on printer, paper size etc.), tell the printer to **spit out the current page and feed through a new one.**

There are special instructions in each computer language to tell the printer to spit out a new page. You would generally say something like:

```
Skip to New Page
```

You also would **add 1 to a line-counter** every time you print a line (write a record).

Straight after this you would check how many lines have printed by seeing the value in the **line-counter**, and based on the value, you may ask for a new page:

To illustrate a typical report scenario, let's extract data from a database and print:

Select all required data (records) From Database
Write (print) record
Add 1 to line-counter
If line-counter > 50
Skip to new page
Endif
Endselect

(Your '*Select .... EndSelect*' will repeat all lines coded in between, for each record selected from the database. In this case all records are selected as there is no '*Where*' clause).

Defining your Print Records

Generally, we can fit about 80 bytes (characters) on one line. The programmer will work out what each line should contain.

Some lines will be header records, i.e.

01-Jan-2008	Sales Report
Item	No. Sold

... and some lines will be detail records:

Balls	*500*
Bats	*200*
Cricket Balls	*300*
Darts	*400*
Trainers	*600*

We need to define the record layout 1st, and then move data into the record's fields. Lines that look the same naturally only need to be defined once.

We would define all the different type of lines we want to print in *Temporary Storage*, and just before printing, **move the entire line to the Record, defined to the 'printer file'**:

Print File	(this is linked to the printer)	
Print-Record	80 Bytes, Alpha	
Temporary Storage		
Header-Record 1		
Date	10 Bytes, Alpha	
Dummy-field	15 bytes, Alpha (spaces)	
Heading1	20 Bytes, Alpha value 'Sales Report'	
Header-Record 2		
Heading2	4 Bytes, Alpha vale 'Item'	
Dummy-field	15 bytes, Alpha (spaces)	
Heading3	8 Bytes, Alpha value 'No. Sold'	
Detail-Record		
Item	20 Bytes, Alpha	
Dummy-field	10 bytes, Alpha (spaces)	
Total	5 Bytes, Numeric	

As discussed above, we would fill the fields of the records with data and then write the records out.

Notice how the fields called **'heading1/2/3'** are defined with the actual words to be used on the header line i.e. *'Sales Report'*.

We have also defined a *'dummy field'* which is used to assign spaces where required on the print line.

We would only need to fill the 'Header-Record' fields with data once, since the fields do not change from page to page. Other reports may need more work on the header if for example, 'Page Number' was needed.

The 'Detail-Record', on the other hand, will be updated with each record we *select* out of the database:

Set Date of Header-Record to Computer Date
Set Header of Header-Record to 'Sales Report'
Select item, total from SalesDatabase
Set Detail-record Item to SalesDatabase Item
Set Detail-record Total to SalesDatabase Total
Write out Print-Record From Detail-Record
Add 1 to line-counter
If line-counter Greater Than 60
Skip to new page
Write Print-Record From Header-Record
Endif
Endselect

Happy Printing!

23) Thorough Testing

This is the ONE MILLION DOLLAR question in the world of programming … **"Have you tested your code properly?"**. Let's discuss this.

Having a look at the below code, it is clear we are reading through a sales file and accumulating totals for each account:

Read 1st record
Do Until all Records Read
Set account-total to 0
Do until account-no changes
Add amount to account-total
Read next record
EndDo
Display account, account-total
EndDo

What would happen if you left out the statement:

Set account-total to 0?

When the 'account' changed, the total would not be reset, so the new account would keep adding to the previous total. This is a typical example of the need to thoroughly test your program with test data.

We so often leave out that one statement that makes such a difference to our results, or we put the statement in the wrong place. We can write a program with hundreds of lines of code and so easily make a mistake. Remember, programming is an exact science – the code has to be 100% correct. On the surface, the code may look perfect but until tested thoroughly you will never know.

The key to thorough testing is setting up test data and running the data through your program. If you are a true programmer, you will run test data through your design on paper 1st, and when happy, will build the code and execute the program with test data.

Everything needs to be tested.

Using your design, you need to take your test data and pass it through each and every line of code.

Once you are happy with your logic you still need to test on the computer. Even after dry running on paper, there could still be other problems not picked up:

> *Perhaps you forgot your 'Read next record' - in which case the tested program would loop.*
>
> *Perhaps you are defining your 'field types' incorrectly in which case a 'Move' statement might crash the program.*
>
> *Perhaps your 'display' or 'printing' is wrong.*

... and so on. There could be one or many errors that can only be picked up through actually executing your program on the machine.

You do not **ever** want to be in a position where you put a program live without testing thoroughly. It will make your work look sloppy, and it might hurt the company.

So … don't panic - just test properly.

24) How to Learn Programming Quickly

One thing you want to strive for is to learn your programming language in as little time as possible. You don't want to be sitting there after 6 months and not be able to finish a program. Here are a few suggestions to get there as quickly as possible.

Master Your Course Material

A great start to your programming career is by completing your course (I assume you will be going on some course) with flying colors. Having lectured programming I can suggest the following:

No messing around in lectures, you need to focus and concentrate.
Things that need explaining need to be written down, you won't remember it.
Don't be afraid to ask questions, but don't hog the lecturer's time either.
Do all your exercises, this is where you learn to program.
Rewrite the notes in your own words, leaving out the nonsense (especially valuable if you will write an exam).
Get a good nights rest every night, and keep your relaxation healthy, you need your brain.

Program Program Program

The quickest way to becoming proficient is to jump right in and get your hands dirty. Like all things in life, practice makes perfect. The more you do the better you get - it's that simple.

You will find the learning curve steep in the beginning but the more you code, the easier it gets. You need to keep 'pushing on' in the beginning and soon enough you will get to a point where you can build code straight from your head.

Get to know your Textbooks

Let's face it, you won't come off course knowing and remembering everything. Hopefully, what you will know is where to find it, and key to this is knowing your textbooks.

The better you know your textbooks the quicker you learn. The trick here is not to know all the content (ideal but unrealistic), but how to find stuff quickly. Again, this will only come from spending time in them, and soon they will become your programming 'friends'.

They give you the correct code and usually accompanying examples, so give it a bash on your own and if there is no success, pull out the books.

Learn to Search on the Web

A great tool available these days is the internet. Time and time again, I use the available search engines to find out how to code something. The key to this tool is using the right search phrase. I always type in **"what I want do"** followed by the programming language e.g.

"Date Validation" COBOL.

25) How to Start Building your Program

In Book I, we likened building a program without a design, to building a house without a plan. Not a good idea.

Program design is key. Design for 3 days and you will code for 3 days. Design for 1 day and you will end up coding for 9 days.

Write out the Specification (requirements)

The 1st step is to have the 'spec' committed to paper. This should detail each and every requirement of the program. The more complex and ambiguous the spec is, the more time you will waste. The trick is to have a very clear and concise explanation of what is required, written out clearly and leaving nothing to memory.

Ponder over a Solution

Read and re-read the spec until you have a complete understanding. Once you are ready to start, don't jump into a solution just yet. Walk around the office, go get a coffee, stare into space and do nothing for a few minutes. Let your sub-conscious start processing a solution. This way you start off relaxed and in control.

Then sit down and start thinking how you are going to tackle the program. Think about the program at large – What is 'input'? What is done with the 'input'? What is 'output'? How is it displayed? … and so on. You still haven't started a solution.

Put Pen to Paper

Make sure you have a few pieces of blank paper in front of you. I **repeat**, a few pieces of blank paper, not 1 piece with a bit of drawing space. Now start from top down, building your design.

Depending on the spec, put down your driving sub-routine names 1st i.e. the routines that will drive your program e.g.

- initialize fields
- **display and process menu**
- display results

This gives you your basic plan to work with.

Drill Down

Now drill down into each sub-routine and detail what needs to be done e.g. 'display and process menu':

- display menu on screen
- get input from user
- when input data, process new-account
- when change data, process **change-account**

Then on a new sheet drill down into each sub-routine e.g. 'change-account':
- get account to change
- display details of account
- select account from table
- update record

Dry Run

This is the most important part of your design. Once you have the full design on paper, 'dry run' the program. This means you start at the top and follow your logic through, taking each and every option available. If you are happy, start coding, if not make your changes and dry run again and again until your code works on paper.

Write out Code (advisable)

This last step is advisable but not essential. It really helps when you have complex code to work through, like 'unloading tables' or complex 'IF' statements. Time and time again I have wasted so much time working out why my program is not producing the required results. If I just wrote my code down in the 1st place, I could have 'dry run' it with test data and seen there and then that it did not work. Don't be lazy.

Then ... HIT THAT KEYBOARD.

26) Programming & Career Options

The world of programming has a multitude of specialties, giving us a wide range of areas in which to focus our careers.

The 2 main choices to make are:

1. Which technology to get involved in?
2. Which work environment would suit you best?

Let's get an **overview** of the technologies out there. We'll discuss work environments thereafter. I've tried to simplify, but it's still quite a bit to take in so it may require a re-read.

PC Programmers

These are the guys that write your mainstream programs that are generally run on desk tops, are interactive and user friendly. You find these programs in the shops behind the counter, at the movie ticket sales, the tellers at the banks, the video store etc. These programs are built to run small businesses or are combined with many other programs to help run larger businesses. Typically used languages are JAVA, C, DELPHI, Visual Basic. The more experienced PC programmers also write cool stuff like games and animation.

Internet Programmers

Internet programmers are the guys that write the fancy stuff on the internet. I am not talking about the fancy graphics with links and display information (which is built by 'web designers'). I am talking about the involved processes that go on behind the scenes like sending information from the web page to a database and back. These guys generally use .NET, ASP, PHP or Coldfusion. These guys not only have to know how to program but also how to incorporate programs into a web site, exciting stuff.

Mainframe Programmers

These guys work for the large companies like banks, insurance companies, and huge retail stores. They write programs that deal with huge amounts of data, like processing millions and millions of customer's information. This stuff needs huge computers to run, called 'mainframes'. A large proportion of programmers fall into this range. Typical languages used are COBOL, DB2 or CICS. A lot of these programs are usually 'back-end' programs that do processing behind the scenes, as oppose to 'front-end' programs that are interactive with a person behind the screen.

Database Specialists

Larger companies that have a massive database infrastructure, employ specialists to look after these databases. After all, this is where all the data is stored. These folks are called Database Administrators (DBA's), and have been trained to handle the 'ins' and 'outs' of storing this data safely and accessing this data easily. They play a huge role in the organization as without the data, we can shut the systems down.

ERP (Enterprise Resource Planning) Specialists

Large businesses are made up of different divisions (sales, accounts, marketing, human resources, stock) each requiring their own processes (programs). The challenge has always been getting these different processes to 'talk' to one another i.e. for the 'sales' programs to feed data to the 'marketing' programs.

ERP systems are very large applications, incorporating all these areas, using the same technology. An example of such an application is *SAP*, and 2 programming languages used to build this application are *ABAP* and *JAVA*. This is not a place to start a programming career as it requires a few years exposure to systems, but definitely where more experienced folk are aiming toward.

Which technology do you think best suits your personality?

The programming world (like most industries) offers 3 main work environments:

- your own business
- working for a small company
- working for a large company

Lets explore each of these.

Own Business

A programming business would generally entail building software for different businesses. Some programming houses focus on one particular area of business (like accounts), and others build software for any area or requirement for any business.

Unless you have some good experience behind you, it is not advisable to start off on your own. Clients will expect you to deliver a perfect solution to meet their business requirement. In order to do this your programming skills must be good enough to deliver the solution from beginning to end. This you can only get through experience.

You will also need to have an understanding of their business to build the correct solution. This knowledge only comes with a little exposure to the business world.

Having said all of this, if you do get your ducks in a row one day and make a go of it, you can be enormously successful and have a huge amount of fun.

Working for a small company

This is a great way to increase your knowledge and gain experience because simply put … they make you do everything.

Although you specialize in programming, you will help out with the network, you get to install and try out different software, and you might help out with a bit of hardware … sort of a 'jack of all trades'. At the end of the day you become well rounded in the high-tech (IT) game which will always stand you in good stead.

As far as programming experience is concerned, you will be pushed to heights you wouldn't have dreamed of. This is largely due the fact that there is not an abundance of programmers to spoon feed you. You have to work stuff out yourself and there is no better way to learn because that way you really understand things.

A huge advantage is that you get to build a lot of software from scratch (development), as oppose to fixing or changing software built by others (maintenance). Sometimes there is no escaping maintenance work, but development work is imperative to becoming an experienced programmer.

Working for large companies

Being in a large company has some amazing benefits:

- you have access to training (in-house and external)

- you have access to many experienced programmers for assistance

- you have access to the latest and greatest software and hardware

- you get to transfer to different programming areas - with time, you have the option of moving from a technical role (programming) to a management role

- some programmers even get to move from high-tech (IT) into the business side of the company

- you get to do both development and maintenance.

Large companies generally have huge software systems that have been developed and improved on over many years. The challenge is getting to know these systems intricately. This requires patience and hard work - again, what you put in is what you get out.

If the corporate world is for you, I believe the trick is to stay with one firm or at least limit your moves from company to company. You can be the greatest programmer in the world but when you move to a new company, you start from scratch in terms of learning their systems and business.

Personally, if the salary meets your requirements, I believe this is the place to be.

I WISH YOU ALL THE VERY BEST IN THE WORLD OF PROGRAMMING.

INDEX

www.ingramcontent.com/pod-product-compliance
Lightning Source LLC
Chambersburg PA
CBHW060455060326
40689CB00020B/4538